D1123395

autumn
cooking

BRIDGET JONES

using the season's finest ingredients

autumn

cooking

LORENZ BOOKS

NOTES

Bracketed terms are intended for American readers.

For all recipes, quantities are given in both metric and imperial measures and, where appropriate, measures are also given in standard cups and spoons. Follow one set, but not a mixture, because they are not interchangeable.

Standard spoon and cup measures are level. 1 tsp = 5ml, 1 tbsp = 15ml, 1 cup = 250ml/8fl oz

Australian standard tablespoons are 20ml. Australian readers should use 3 tsp in place of 1 tbsp for measuring small quantities of gelatine, flour, salt, etc.

Medium (US large) eggs are used unless otherwise stated.

Please note that the publisher cannot accept responsibility for any illness caused by eating wild produce. Please consult an authoritative guide before eating mushrooms.

This edition is published by Lorenz Books

Lorenz Books is an imprint of Anness Publishing Ltd
Hermes House, 88–89 Blackfriars Road, London SE1 8HA
tel. 020 7401 2077; fax 020 7633 9499
www.lorenzbooks.com; info@anness.com

© Anness Publishing Ltd 2003

This edition distributed in the UK by The Manning Partnership Ltd, 6 The Old Dairy
Melcombe Road, Bath BA2 3LR; tel. 01225 478 444; fax 01225 478 440
sales@manning-partnership.co.uk

This edition distributed in the USA and Canada by National Book Network
4501 Forbes Boulevard, Suite 200, Lanham, MD 20706; tel. 301 459 3366; fax 301 429 5746;
www.nbnbooks.com

This edition distributed in Australia by Pan Macmillan Australia, Level 18, St Martins Tower
31 Market St, Sydney, NSW 2000; tel. 1300 135 113; fax 1300 135 103
customer.service@macmillan.com.au

This edition distributed in New Zealand by David Bateman Ltd, 30 Tarndale Grove
Off Bush Road, Albany, Auckland; tel. (09) 415 7664; fax (09) 415 8892

All rights reserved. No part of this publication may be reproduced, stored in a retrieval system, or transmitted in any way or by any means, electronic, mechanical, photocopying, recording or otherwise, without the prior written permission of the copyright holder.

A CIP catalogue record for this book is available from the British Library.

PUBLISHER: Joanna Lorenz
MANAGING EDITOR: Judith Simons
PROJECT EDITOR: Katy Bevan
EDITORIAL ASSISTANT: Lindsay Kaubi
DESIGNER: Adelle Morris
EDITORIAL READER: Lindsay Zamponi
PRODUCTION CONTROLLER: Darren Price
PHOTOGRAPHERS: Peter Anderson, Martin Brigdale, James Duncan, Gus Filgate, Michelle Garrett, Don Last, William Lingwood, Patrick McLeavey, Thomas Odulate, Craig Robertson, Jo Whitworth
RECIPES: Maxine Clark, Joanna Farrow, Christine Ingram, Lucy Knox, Keith Richmond, Rena Salaman, Simon Smith, Ysanne Spevack, Linda Tubby, Steven Wheeler

10 9 8 7 6 5 4 3 2 1

CONTENTS

INTRODUCTION

As bright summer hues mellow to a glow, the flavours and aromas of produce seem to mature to a rounded richness. Sedate autumn provides a harvest of fruit, vegetables and leaves that is less demanding than the fast-growing summer glut. There are plump, crisp cabbages; firm roots and tubers; crunchy apples and juicy pears. In many rural areas astounding pyramids of golden pumpkins take on sculptural forms at farm gates and in farmers' markets. Slightly smaller pumpkins and squashes make a correspondingly dramatic impact on supermarket displays.

Against a backcloth of smoke from gently smouldering leaves, gardeners unearth substantial root vegetables. The weather is perfect for pottering in the kitchen garden – neither hot enough to laze, nor cold enough for hand-clapping and foot-stamping. The tangled remnants of summer growth are cleared to reveal big vegetables and firm fruit with well-defined flavours – perfect for complementing the season's meats.

For food shopping, the change from summer to autumn is a metamorphosis rather than a sudden switch. Chunky root vegetables become affordable, and there is a good choice of apples and pears from local orchards. Supermarket meat displays offer braising and stewing cuts, while butchers dealing in game display the new season's birds to good effect in their windows.

Warming dishes

One of the pleasures of autumn cooking is its relaxed pace, when evenings at home begin to seem like a good idea. Warmer foods become appealing – mellow casseroles, creamy mash, moist risottos, baked soufflés and soothing soups. It may not yet be cool enough for steaming porridge, but warm buns and breads are welcome alternatives or additions to breakfast fruit salads and yogurts. Country walks provide opportunities for

rummaging among the brambles for juicy fruit, gathering nuts and picking mushrooms. Traditionally, going home for tea meant that there was probably teabread or fruit loaf to sample, because autumn is the time of year when there is renewed enthusiasm for baking, keeping the house warm with a constant supply of heat and delicious aromas.

Seasonal celebrations

A good harvest is usually celebrated by sharing meals and distributing produce to the community. Festivities take over on Halloween, bonfire night and Thanksgiving, providing opportunities for fun parties. Fancy dress or cool-weather barbecues are informal, with sizzling-hot sausages and chargrilled baked potatoes accompanied by steaming mugs of golden pumpkin soup. Toffee apples, gooey apple cakes and oaty flapjacks are sweet treats.

Storing for winter

Autumn is the time for squirrelling away winter stores. Pickles and chutneys are just right for using apples, pears, crisp red cabbage and those leftover tomatoes that will not ripen on the windowsill. Chutneys, pickles and clear jellies, made from quinces or crab apples, for instance, are the perfect complement to cold meat cuts and cheeses.

A glut of apples or pears can be preserved by wrapping each fruit in paper and storing in a cool and dark place. Root vegetables can be saved in sand or sawdust. Onions and garlic bulbs can be strung up and hung for use even later in the year. Stringing is an excellent way to ensure that alliums stay dry and well ventilated, and it will keep them for use in the following spring if kept in a frost-free place.

Hedgerow pickings

One of the traditional pleasures of autumn is the gathering of nature's free harvest. Country dwellers have long benefited from fruit from the hedgerows and fungi from the ground. Domestic traditions for when and how to pick are passed down through generations and matched by recipes for jams and pickles.

FINE FRUIT

Prize pickings are found high on the hedges and branches exposed to the sun. The right rainfall produces plump fruit – succulent blackberries on tangled brambles; bright clusters of rowan berries high in mountain ash trees; glowing rose hips on thorny climbers; and astringent little wild crab apples. The best and sweetest blackberries are big and tender, and they taste wonderful freshly picked, with sugar and cream. They can also be poached, used in baked desserts or made into jams and jellies.

Rowan berries, rose hips and crab apples throw off their bitter guise and burst into flavour when cooked or crushed. Straining and sweetening releases and enhances the fruity essence, which is superb in syrups and preserves. Sour sloes and tart damsons also taste fabulous in all sorts of cooked dishes. Sloe gin is especially good: each fruit has to be well pricked (traditionally, with a silver needle) before being macerated in spirit.

NICE NUTS

Trees laden with hazelnuts are irresistible to wildlife and human gatherers alike. Those who are accustomed to spotting the little clusters of brown shells hidden between speckled leaves usually enjoy them young, crisp and moist, while they are still slightly under-ripe. Any nuts that survive undiscovered on the branches to mature are fuller in flavour. They can be stored in cool, dry conditions for later in the year.

MARVELLOUS MUSHROOMS

Wild mushrooms seem to make a miraculous appearance in autumn. When the weather is just right – neither too wet, nor too dry – weird and wonderful fungi seem to grow almost overnight, ready to be plucked with care from open fields or from beneath the ground cover of autumn leaves.

Experienced fungi foragers exercise knowledge and respect, understanding that many edible fungi are partnered by poisonous look-alikes. They treat each species with care, selecting only the examples they know to be safe. And the crop is always respected, never ravaged, for rough lifting and overpicking destroy the fragile equilibrium of renewal. Please consult an authoritative guide before eating any fungi.

Preparing wild mushrooms requires a little patience to remove dirt. This involves gently wiping, cleaning with a soft brush, or swirling in water, but never soaking. A network of tiny holes is the tell-tale sign that bugs may be present; trimming off small areas usually disposes of unwanted pests. Fungi that are riddled with holes must be discarded, so the trick is to spot bad attacks while picking and leave the fungi in the wild to grow and reproduce.

Drying is one method of preserving wild mushrooms. The traditional method is to thread the mushrooms on string and hang them in a dry, warm and airy place to dry slowly. They can also be dried in electric fan-assisted dryers or on racks in a very cool oven. To store the fungi in a container (rather than strung up in a suitable area), they must be thoroughly dried or they will go mouldy. When completely dry, they can be stored in airtight containers in a cool, dark cupboard indefinitely.

Drying changes the character of wild fungi ingredients, transforming them from lightly flavoured foods requiring minimal cooking, to concentrated ingredients with condiment-like qualities. Dried mushrooms can bring an intense richness to sauces, casseroles and risottos.

Harvest highlights

Orchard fruit, squashes and grains are good at this time of year and pumpkins are an essential feature. Large main crop potatoes have thick skins that become deliciously crisp when baked; with buttery, fluffy centres, they are a firm favourite.

TERRIFIC ROOTS AND STEMS

Main-crop carrots, swedes (rutabagas) and the first of the parsnips are piled on vegetable stalls and in supermarkets. However, traditionally parsnips are not considered to be at their best until they have had a dose of frost in the ground. Celeriac and Jerusalem artichokes are two delicately flavoured ground vegetables to seek out.

Celeriac is not strictly a root but the swollen stem base (or corm) of the plant. It has a mild celery flavour and a slightly crunchy texture. The large, unevenly surfaced bulb should be peeled and then sliced or diced for cooking. It is good raw or cooked, especially in soup, puréed or poached in a little white wine and stock. Boil and mash celeriac with potatoes to make a creamy accompaniment for grilled fish.

Jerusalem artichokes are also delicate, but with a nutty flavour. They are incredibly easy to grow and provide a generous crop. Modern cultivars are not as rugged and knobbly as the older ones, so they are easier to scrub. The flesh is crisp and rather thin in texture, becoming watery if overcooked. Jerusalem artichokes have a reputation for causing flatulence, especially when made into soup. This is because they contain inulin, a type of fructose that is indigestible. Inulin is soluble, so some is lost in discarded cooking water but, of course, not when both vegetables and cooking liquid make soup. The flavour may be splendid, but to those who find artichokes a problem, the side effects are unpleasant. Parboiling in their skins, then tossing with a little oil and roasting works well. Peeling and simmering for five minutes before slicing is another good starting point. The slices are delicious sautéed or drizzled with a little cream, sprinkled lightly with breadcrumbs and baked until golden.

IMPRESSIVE PUMPKINS

Many people are intimidated by the sheer size of pumpkins and afraid they may run short of ideas or tire of pumpkin pie or soup. There is no need to worry though, as the pumpkin is such a versatile vegetable. There will always be extra to cook with after the traditional lanterns have been carved.

- Slice the top off a small pumpkin and scoop out the seeds. Replace the top and bake, wrapped in foil. Scoop out and purée the tender flesh with good stock and cream to make a silky soup. Reheat without boiling, then season with snipped chives and nutmeg.

- Steam or boil wedges or cubes of pumpkin until just tender for bakes, gratins and pies. Cook until soft for purée. Add to vegetable stews and serve with couscous.

- Diced pumpkin makes excellent chutney or pickle.

GOOD SEEDS AND GRAINS

There are lots of delicious ways to use oats, barley, wheat and rye flakes, not just in baking breads and cakes. Containing the vitamins and minerals found in most seeds, they provide a healthy complement to any diet.

- Dry-roast flaked grains in a heavy pan over a low heat, stirring until lightly browned. Cook each type separately, then mix together. Roast sesame, sunflower and pumpkin seeds in separate batches and add to the grains. Use in muesli (granola), bread doughs, as a gratin topping, in salads or sprinkled over soup.

- Add oat flakes to crumble mix for topping apples or other fruit.

- Rolled or flaked oats are convenient and easy for thickening soup. Stir them into the soup while bringing to the boil. Simmer for a few minutes, until thick.

APPLES AND PEARS

Cooking apples become soft and pulpy during cooking. They are good for apple sauce, purée and chutney. Dessert apples become tender but stay whole when cooked. They are good poached, baked or used in tarte tatin. Apples and pears discolour quickly when cut and peeled. To prevent this, place the fruit in a bowl of water with a good squeeze of lemon juice.

- Poach halved, peeled and cored dessert apples in cider syrup with 3-4 green cardamom pods until tender. Reduce the syrup to a small amount of golden glaze to coat the apples before serving warm.

- Poach whole, peeled dessert apples or pears until tender. Cool, then drain, and remove their cores. Fill the cavity with marzipan, wrap in filo pastry and bake until crisp and golden.

Seasonal bakes

Hearty breads and flavour-packed preserves are signature dishes of the season. Together they complement hard or soft cheese, baked ham and cured meats. Sweet-sour pickles and crusty bread also go very well with thick seasonal soups.

RAISING BREAD

The aroma of freshly baked bread, raised with yeast, is unbeatable. There are several types of yeast. Fresh yeast is beige and moist but firm, with a crumbly "squeaky" texture – it is mixed with a little warm liquid and allowed to become frothy before it is added to the dough. The dough must rise twice. Ordinary dried yeast is sprinkled over warm liquid and allowed to rehydrate and become frothy. Fast-action dried yeast is added to dry ingredients. Instead of the traditional double rising, the dough is shaped and allowed to prove or rise once only.

- Use milk instead of water to make a slightly richer bread with a deep golden crust.

- Soda bread is quick and easy. Bicarbonate of soda (baking soda) is used as the raising agent, with buttermilk to mix or lemon juice added to the dough.

- Savoury scone (biscuit) dough uses baking powder or a mixture of bicarbonate of soda and cream of tartar as a raising agent. Mixed dried herbs or oregano and finely chopped sundried tomatoes taste good in scones, especially with a little freshly grated Parmesan.

- Packet dough mix is a good base for flavoured bread. Add roasted fennel or caraway seeds to white bread mix or chopped walnuts to wholemeal (whole-wheat) mix.

- Add mixed dried fruit to dough to transform plain bread into a fruit loaf.

Preserving

Chutneys and pickles are hassle-free preserves – easy to make, safe to store and versatile in use. They are convenient storecupboard condiments and well suited to contemporary cooking and eating.

Vinegar and sugar are the preserving agents. Classic chutneys are simmered gently for hours until thick and pulpy. Pickles are cooked for a shorter period, until tender but still chunky. Some pickles are simply raw or poached fruit or vegetables immersed in vinegar or vinegar syrup; the pickling liquor is not consumed.

Whole or ground spices are typical flavouring ingredients – coriander, cloves, allspice, fennel seeds, chillies and/or ground ginger. Onions are essential, garlic is widely used, and fresh root ginger occasionally contributes its inimitable zest.

- Whole spices contribute a cleaner flavour than their ground counterparts. Tie them in a piece of muslin to remove them easily from a pickle or chutney after cooking. Crushed spices and small whole seeds contribute texture to pickles.

- For smooth, mellow chutneys, simmer the mixture gently until soft before adding the sugar, then continue cooking very slowly until rich and thick.

- The longer the preserve is cooked once the sugar is added, the richer, darker and more caramelized it becomes.

- Dried fruit, such as dates, raisins and apricots, are used whole, chunky or chopped for their flavour and sweetness.

STORING, MATURING AND USING

Pots with vinegar-proof lids are essential, otherwise the vinegar attacks and breaks down exposed metal, spoiling the preserve. Jars should be thoroughly washed in sterilizing solution and warmed. Pot cooked preserves immediately, covering them while they are red hot for a good, clean seal.

All chutneys and pickles should be matured for at least a couple of weeks before eating, preferably for one month. As the vinegar and spices mellow, the preserve becomes less harsh and more intriguing in flavour. Stored in a cool, dark and dry place, they keep for 6–12 months.

- Serve preserves with cheese and cooked meats. Spread them in sandwiches – sweet-sour pickle goes especially well with smooth peanut butter.

- Offer chunky pumpkin pickle with rich patés or terrines.

- Ginger-seasoned pickles are good with roasted carrots or swirled into smooth, rich carrot or parsnip soup.

- Light pickles, with the sugar added fairly late in the cooking process, are delicious in salad dressings for chunks of cooked chicken or ham.

warm and comforting

As autumn arrives and the days get shorter and cooler, relaxing meals at home become appealing. The season has come for curling up with warm, comforting food after a country walk or afternoons spent in the garden tending a bonfire. Enjoy hearty soups, savoury pastries and pâtés, warm salads and hot seafood as appetizers or as satisfying side dishes.

Lentils are an autumn staple. As they do not need soaking, they make an easy option for a quick meal. The secret of good lentil soup is to be generous with the olive oil.

LENTIL and TOMATO SOUP

INGREDIENTS
serves four

275g | 10oz | 1¼ cups brown-green lentils, preferably the small variety

150ml | ¼ pint | ⅔ cup extra virgin olive oil

1 onion, thinly sliced

2 garlic cloves, sliced into thin batons

1 carrot, sliced into thin discs

400g | 14oz can chopped tomatoes

15ml | 1 tbsp tomato purée (paste)

2.5ml | ½ tsp dried oregano

1 litre | 1¾ pints | 4 cups hot water

salt and ground black pepper

30ml | 2 tbsp roughly chopped fresh herb leaves, to garnish

1 Rinse the lentils, drain them and put them in a large pan with cold water to cover. Bring to the boil and boil for 3–4 minutes. Strain, discarding the liquid, and set the lentils aside.

2 Wipe the pan clean, heat the olive oil in it, then add the onion and sauté until translucent. Stir in the garlic and, as soon as it becomes aromatic, return the lentils to the pan. Add the carrot, tomatoes, tomato purée and oregano. Stir in the hot water and a little pepper to taste.

3 Bring to the boil, then lower the heat, cover the pan and cook gently for 20–30 minutes until the lentils feel soft but have not begun to disintegrate. Add salt and the chopped herbs just before serving.

COOK'S TIP This recipe uses staples from the pantry. Serve with fresh warm bread and cheese to complement the flavours and to make a filling and hearty meal. If you still have a few remaining herbs in the kitchen garden, such as sage or rosemary, these can be used to replace the dried oregano.

This silky, smooth and nutty soup with hints of smoky bacon is so easy to make. Enjoy it with a bowl of warmed tortilla chips, spiced-up with extra paprika and cumin.

BACON and CHICKPEA SOUP

1 Drain the chickpeas, put them in a large pan and cover with plenty of cold water. Bring to the boil and simmer for about 20 minutes. Strain and set aside.

2 Melt the butter in a large pan and add the pancetta or streaky bacon. Fry over a medium heat until just beginning to turn golden. Add the chopped vegetables and cook for 5–10 minutes until soft.

3 Add the chickpeas to the pan, with the chopped rosemary, bay leaves, halved garlic cloves and enough water to cover completely. Bring to the boil, half cover, turn down the heat and simmer for 45–60 minutes, stirring occasionally. (The chickpeas should start to disintegrate and will thicken the soup.)

4 Allow the soup to cool slightly, then pour it into a blender or food processor and process until smooth. Return the soup to the rinsed-out pan, taste and season with salt and plenty of black pepper. Reheat gently.

5 To make the tortilla chips, preheat the oven to 180°C | 350°F | Gas 4. Melt the butter with the paprika and cumin in a pan, then lightly brush the mixture over the tortilla chips. Reserve any left over spiced butter. Spread the chips out on a baking sheet and warm through in the oven for 5 minutes.

6 Ladle the soup into bowls, pour some reserved spiced butter over each serving and sprinkle with a little paprika. Serve with the warm tortilla chips.

INGREDIENTS
serves four to six

400g | 14oz | 2 cups dried chickpeas, soaked overnight in cold water

115g | 4oz | ½ cup butter

150g | 5oz pancetta or streaky (fatty) *(Tofu)* bacon, roughly chopped

2 onions, finely chopped

1 carrot, chopped

1 celery stick, chopped

15ml | 1 tbsp chopped fresh rosemary

2 fresh bay leaves

2 garlic cloves, halved

salt and ground black pepper

for the tortilla chips

75g | 3oz | 6 tbsp butter

2.5ml | ½ tsp sweet paprika

1.5ml | ¼ tsp ground cumin

175g | 6oz plain tortilla chips

Pine nuts are the seeds that come from the cones of the pinus pinea tree. Their delicate nutty taste is a marvellous foil to the feta cheese in these parcels. Offer round with drinks or present as part of a large meal or buffet table.

HALF-MOON CHEESE PIES with PINE NUTS

INGREDIENTS
makes twelve to fourteen

1 large (US extra large) egg, plus 1 egg yolk for glazing

150g | 5oz feta cheese

30ml | 2 tbsp milk

30ml | 2 tbsp chopped fresh mint leaves

15ml | 1 tbsp raisins

15 ml | 1 tbsp pine nuts, lightly toasted

a little vegetable oil, for greasing

for the pastry

225g | 8oz | 2 cups self-raising (self-rising) flour

45ml | 3 tbsp extra virgin olive oil

15g | 1/2oz | 1 tbsp butter, melted

90g | 31/2oz Greek (strained plain) yogurt

1 To make the pastry, put the flour in a bowl and mix in the oil, butter and yogurt by hand. Cover and rest in the refrigerator for 15 minutes.

2 Meanwhile, make the filling. Beat the egg lightly in a bowl. Crumble in the cheese, then mix in the milk, mint, raisins and pine nuts.

3 Preheat the oven to 190°C | 375°F | Gas 5. Cover half of the pastry, thinly roll out the remainder and cut out 7.5cm | 3in rounds.

4 Place a heaped teaspoon of filling on each round and fold the pastry over to make a half-moon shape. Press the edges to seal, then place the pies on a greased baking sheet. Repeat with the remaining pastry. Brush the pies with egg yolk and bake for 20 minutes, or until golden.

This pâté is particularly good made with the new season's walnuts, sometimes known as "wet" walnuts, which are available in the early autumn.

ROAST GARLIC with GOAT'S CHEESE PÂTÉ

1 Preheat the oven to 180°C|350°F|Gas 4. Strip the papery skin from the garlic bulbs. Place them in an ovenproof dish large enough to hold them snugly. Tuck in the fresh rosemary sprigs and fresh thyme sprigs, drizzle the olive oil over and season with a little sea salt and plenty of ground black pepper.

2 Cover the garlic tightly with foil and bake in the oven for 50–60 minutes, opening the parcel and basting once halfway through the cooking time. Set aside and leave to cool.

3 Preheat the grill (broiler). To make the pâté, cream the cheese with the thyme, parsley and chopped walnuts. Beat in 15ml|1 tbsp of the cooking oil from the garlic and season to taste with plenty of ground black pepper. Transfer the pâté to a serving bowl and chill until ready to serve.

4 Brush the sourdough bread slices on one side with the remaining cooking oil from the garlic bulbs, then grill (broil) until lightly toasted.

5 Divide the pâté among four individual plates. Drizzle the walnut oil, if using, over the goat's cheese pâté and grind some black pepper over it. Place some garlic on each plate and serve with the pâté and some toasted bread. Garnish the pâté with a little fresh thyme and serve a few freshly shelled walnuts with each portion.

INGREDIENTS
serves four

4 large garlic bulbs

4 fresh rosemary sprigs

8 fresh thyme sprigs

60ml|4 tbsp olive oil

sea salt and ground black pepper

thyme sprigs, to garnish

4–8 slices sourdough bread and walnuts, to serve

for the pâté

200g|7oz|scant 1 cup soft goat's cheese

5ml|1 tsp finely chopped fresh thyme

15ml|1 tbsp chopped fresh parsley

50g|2oz|1/3 cup chopped walnuts

15ml|1 tbsp walnut oil (optional)

fresh thyme, to garnish

Shallot and chives in a creamy dressing add bite to this warm salad of potato and sweet mussels. Serve with a bowl of full-flavoured watercress and plenty of freshly baked wholewheat bread for perfect autumn fare.

POTATO and MUSSEL SALAD

INGREDIENTS
serves four

675g | 1¹/₂lb salad potatoes

1kg | 2¹/₄lb mussels, scrubbed and beards removed

200ml | 7fl oz | scant 1 cup dry white wine

15g | ¹/₂oz flat leaf parsley, chopped

salt and ground black pepper

chopped fresh chives or chive flowers, to garnish

for the dressing

105ml | 7 tbsp mild olive oil

15–30ml | 1–2 tbsp white wine vinegar

5ml | 1 tsp Dijon mustard

1 large shallot, very finely chopped

15ml | 1 tbsp chopped fresh chives

45ml | 3 tbsp double (heavy) cream

pinch of sugar (optional)

1 Cook the potatoes whole in boiling, salted water for 15–20 minutes or until tender. Drain, cool, then peel. Slice the potatoes into a bowl and toss with 30ml | 2 tbsp of the oil for the dressing.

2 Discard any open mussels that do not close when sharply tapped. Bring the white wine to the boil in a large, heavy pan. Add the mussels, cover and boil vigorously for 3–4 minutes, shaking the pan occasionally, until the mussels have opened. Discard any mussels that have not opened after 5 minutes' cooking. Drain and shell the mussels, reserving the cooking liquid.

3 Boil the reserved cooking liquid until reduced to about 45ml | 3tbsp. Strain this through a fine sieve over the potatoes and toss to mix.

4 For the dressing, whisk together the remaining oil, 15ml | 1tbsp of vinegar, the mustard, shallot and chives.

5 Add the cream and whisk again to form a thick dressing. Adjust the seasoning, adding more vinegar and/or a pinch of sugar to taste.

6 Toss the mussels with the potatoes, then mix in the dressing and chopped parsley. Serve sprinkled with extra chopped chives or chive flowers separated into florets.

COOK'S TIP Potato salads such as this one should not be chilled, as the cold alters the texture of the potatoes and of the creamy dressing. For the best flavour and texture, serve this salad at room temperature.

This is the perfect autumn oyster dish, served bubbling and golden brown. Those who are not "as rich as Rockefeller" can give mussels or clams the same treatment.

OYSTERS ROCKEFELLER

1 Preheat the oven to 220°C | 425°F | Gas 7. Make a bed of coarse salt on two large baking sheets. Set the oysters in the half-shell in the bed of salt to keep them steady. Set aside.

2 Melt the butter in a frying pan. Add the finely chopped shallots and cook them over a low heat for 2–3 minutes until they are softened. Stir in the spinach and let it wilt.

3 Add the parsley, celery leaves and breadcrumbs to the pan and fry gently for 5 minutes. Season with salt, pepper and Tabasco or cayenne.

4 Divide the stuffing among the oysters. Drizzle a few drops of Pernod or Ricard over each oyster, then bake for about 5 minutes, until bubbling and golden brown. Serve on a heated platter on a shallow salt bed with lemon wedges.

COOK'S TIP If you prefer a smoother stuffing, whizz it to a paste in a food processor or blender.

INGREDIENTS
serves six

450g | 1lb | 3 cups coarse salt, plus extra to serve

24 oysters, opened

115g | 4oz | 1/2 cup butter

2 shallots, finely chopped

500g | 1¼lb spinach leaves, finely chopped

60ml | 4 tbsp chopped fresh parsley

60ml | 4 tbsp chopped celery leaves

90ml | 6 tbsp fresh white breadcrumbs

Tabasco sauce or cayenne pepper

10-20ml | 2–4 tsp Pernod or Ricard

salt and ground black pepper

lemon wedges, to serve

earthy and delicious

The richness of autumnal colour is captured in the ripe pumpkins and squashes which appear in heaps in gardens, markets and local shops. Wild mushrooms offer their intense flavour to soufflés and pasta dishes. Chunky root vegetables are abundant too, and they combine brilliantly with the nuttiness of pulses, grains and slowly cooked and caramelized onions or shallots to provide delicious vegetarian options.

The rosemary gives this rich and creamy risotto a sweet pungency, while garlic and chilli add bite.

PUMPKIN, ROSEMARY and CHILLI RISOTTO

INGREDIENTS
serves four

115g | 4oz | 1/2 cup butter

1 small onion, finely chopped

2 large garlic cloves, crushed

1 fresh red chilli, seeded and finely chopped

250g | 9oz | fresh pumpkin or butternut squash, peeled and roughly chopped

30ml | 2 tbsp chopped fresh rosemary

250g | 9oz | 1 1/2 cups risotto rice, preferably Arborio or Vialone Nano

about 750ml | 1 1/4 pints | 3 cups hot chicken stock, preferably fresh

50g | 2oz | 2/3 cup freshly grated Parmesan cheese, plus extra to serve

salt and ground black pepper

1 Melt half the butter in a heavy pan, add the onion and garlic and cook for 10 minutes until softening. Add the chilli and cook for about 1 minute. Add the pumpkin or squash and cook, stirring constantly, for 5 minutes. Stir in the rosemary.

2 Add the rice and stir with a wooden spoon to coat with the oil and vegetables. Cook for 2–3 minutes to toast the rice grains.

3 Begin to add the stock, a large ladleful at a time, stirring all the time until each ladleful has been absorbed into the rice. The rice should always be bubbling slowly. If not, add some more stock. Continue adding the stock like this, until the rice is tender and creamy, but the grains remain firm, and the pumpkin is beginning to disintegrate. (This should take about 20 minutes, depending on the type of rice used.) Taste and season well with salt and pepper.

4 Stir the remaining butter and the cheese into the rice. Cover and allow to rest for 2–3 minutes, then serve straight away with extra Parmesan cheese.

This is more like a nutty pilaf than a classic risotto. Sweet leeks and roasted squash are superb with pearl barley and garlicky mushrooms.

BARLEY RISOTTO with ROASTED SQUASH

1 Rinse and drain the barley. Bring a pan of water to simmering point, add the barley and half-cover. Cook for 35–45 minutes, or until tender. Drain. Preheat the oven to 200°C|400°F|Gas 6.

2 Place the squash in a roasting pan with half the thyme. Season with pepper and toss with half the oil. Roast, stirring once, for 30–35 minutes, until tender and beginning to brown.

3 Heat half the butter with the remaining oil in a large frying pan. Cook the leeks and garlic gently for 5 minutes. Add the mushrooms and remaining thyme, then cook until the liquid from the mushrooms evaporates and the mushrooms begin to fry.

4 Stir in the carrots and cook for 2 minutes, then add the barley and most of the stock. Season and partially cover. Cook for 5 minutes. Pour in the remaining stock if necessary. Stir in the parsley, the remaining butter and half the Pecorino, then the squash, with salt and pepper to taste. Serve, sprinkled with pumpkin seeds and the remaining Pecorino.

INGREDIENTS
serves four to five

200g | 7oz | scant 1 cup pearl barley

1 butternut squash, peeled, seeded and cut into chunks

10ml | 2 tsp chopped fresh thyme

60ml | 4 tbsp olive oil

25g | 1oz | 2 tbsp butter

4 leeks, cut diagonally into fairly thick slices

2 garlic cloves, finely chopped

175g | 6oz | 2 1/4 cups chestnut mushrooms, sliced

2 carrots, coarsely grated

about 120ml | 4fl oz | 1/2 cup vegetable stock

30ml | 2 tbsp chopped fresh flat leaf parsley

50g | 2oz | 1/4 cup Pecorino cheese, grated or shaved

45ml | 3 tbsp pumpkin seeds, toasted

salt and ground black pepper

You can serve this dish as a vegetarian meal on its own, as a side dish or as a topping for couscous. A dollop of garlic-flavoured yogurt or a spoonful of harisssa goes very well with the squash and shallots. Serve this dish with a green salad for supper.

BUTTERNUT SQUASH with PINK SHALLOTS

INGREDIENTS
serves four

900g | 2lb peeled butternut squash, cut into thick slices

120ml | 4fl oz | 1/2 cup water

45–60ml | 3–4 tbsp olive oil

knob (pat) of butter

16–20 pink shallots, peeled

10–12 garlic cloves, peeled

115g/ | 4oz | 1 cup blanched almonds

75g | 3oz | generous 1/2 cup raisins or sultanas (golden raisins), soaked in warm water for 15 minutes and drained

30–45ml | 2–3 tbsp clear honey

10ml | 2 tsp ground cinnamon

small bunch of mint, chopped

salt and ground black pepper

1 lemon, cut into wedges, to serve

1 Preheat the oven to 200°C | 400°F | Gas 6. Place the butternut squash in an ovenproof dish, add the water, cover and bake for about 45 minutes, until tender.

2 Meanwhile, heat the olive oil and butter in a large heavy pan. Stir in the shallots and cook until they begin to brown. Stir in the garlic and almonds.

3 When the garlic and almonds begin to brown, add the raisins or sultanas. Continue to cook until the shallots and garlic begin to caramelize, then stir in the honey and cinnamon, adding a little water if the mixture becomes too dry. Season well with salt and pepper and remove from the heat.

4 Cover the squash with the shallot and garlic mixture and return to the oven, uncovered, for a further 15 minutes. Sprinkle with fresh mint and serve with lemon wedges for squeezing over the vegetables.

COOK'S TIP When in season, substitute pumpkin for the squash.

Wild mushrooms combine especially well with eggs and spinach in this sensational soufflé. Almost any combination of mushrooms can be used for this recipe, although the firmer varieties provide the best texture.

SPINACH and WILD MUSHROOM SOUFFLÉ

INGREDIENTS
serves four

225g | 8oz fresh spinach, washed, or 115g | 4oz frozen chopped spinach

60ml | 4 tbsp unsalted (sweet) butter, plus extra for greasing

1 garlic clove, crushed

175g | 6oz | 1¾ cups assorted wild mushrooms such as ceps, bay boletes, saffron milk-caps, oyster, field mushrooms and hen of the woods, roughly chopped

250ml | 8fl oz | 1 cup milk

45ml | 3 tbsp plain (all-purpose) flour

6 eggs, separated

pinch grated nutmeg

175g | 6oz | 2 cups freshly grated Parmesan cheese

salt and ground black pepper

1 Preheat the oven to 190°C | 375°F | Gas 5. Steam the spinach over a moderate heat for 3–4 minutes. Cool under running water, then drain. Press out as much liquid as you can with the back of a large spoon and chop finely. If using frozen spinach, defrost and squeeze dry in the same way.

2 Gently sauté the garlic and mushrooms in the butter. Turn up the heat and evaporate the juices. When dry, add the spinach and transfer to a bowl. Cover and keep warm.

3 Measure 45ml | 3 tbsp of the milk into a bowl. Bring the remainder to a boil. Stir the flour and egg yolks into the milk in the bowl and blend well. Stir the boiling milk into the egg and flour mixture, return to the pan and simmer to thicken. Add the spinach mixture. Season to taste with salt, pepper and nutmeg.

4 Butter a 900ml | 1½ pints | 3¾ cups soufflé dish, paying attention to the sides. Sprinkle with a little of the cheese. Set aside.

5 Whisk the egg whites until they hold soft peaks. Bring the spinach mixture back to a boil. Stir in a spoonful of beaten egg white, then fold the mixture into the remaining egg white. Turn into the soufflé dish, spread level, sprinkle with the remaining cheese and bake in the oven for about 25 minutes until puffed, risen and golden.

COOK'S TIP The soufflé mixture, up to step 4, can be prepared up to 12 hours in advance and reheated before the beaten egg whites are folded in.

In autumn, thoughts turn to hearty, satisfying food. This sustaining, yet low-fat dish is the ideal choice.

CASSEROLE with HARVEST VEGETABLES

1 Preheat the oven to 180°C|350°F|Gas 4. Heat the oil in a large, flameproof casserole. Add the leeks, garlic and celery and cook over a low heat, stirring occasionally, for 3 minutes, until the leeks begin to soften.

2 Add the carrots, parsnips, sweet potato, swede, lentils, tomatoes, herbs and stock. Stir well and season with salt and pepper to taste. Bring to the boil, stirring occasionally.

3 Cover the casserole, put it in the oven and bake for about 50 minutes, until the vegetables and lentils are tender, stirring the vegetable mixture once or twice.

4 Remove the casserole from the oven. Blend the cornflour with the water in a small bowl. Stir the mixture into the casserole and heat it gently on top of the stove, stirring continuously, until the mixture boils and thickens. Lower the heat and simmer gently for 2 minutes, stirring.

5 Spoon on to warmed serving plates or into bowls, garnish with the thyme sprigs and serve.

INGREDIENTS
serves six

15ml | 1 tbsp sunflower oil

2 leeks, sliced

1 garlic clove, crushed

4 celery sticks, chopped

2 carrots, sliced

2 parsnips, diced

1 sweet potato, diced

225g | 8oz swede, diced

175g | 6oz | 3/4 cup whole brown or green lentils

450g | 1lb tomatoes, peeled, seeded and chopped

15ml | 1 tbsp chopped fresh thyme

15ml | 1 tbsp chopped fresh marjoram

900ml | 1 1/2 pints | 3 3/4 cups vegetable stock

15ml | 1 tbsp cornflour (cornstarch)

45ml | 3 tbsp water

salt and ground black pepper

fresh thyme sprigs, to garnish

The slightly smoky and earthy flavour of Jerusalem artichokes is excellent with shallots and smoked bacon. This dish makes a delicious accompaniment to chicken, roast cod or monkfish, or pork.

JERUSALEM ARTICHOKES with BACON

INGREDIENTS
serves four

50ml | 2fl oz | 1/4 cup butter

115g | 4oz smoked bacon or pancetta, chopped

800g | 1³/4lb Jerusalem artichokes, peeled

8–12 garlic cloves, peeled

115g | 4oz shallots, chopped

75ml | 5 tbsp water

30ml | 2 tbsp olive oil

120ml | 4fl oz | 1/2 cup fresh white breadcrumbs

30-45ml/2–3 tbsp chopped fresh parsley

salt and ground black pepper

1 Melt half the butter in a heavy frying pan and cook the chopped bacon or pancetta until brown and beginning to crisp. Remove half the bacon or pancetta from the pan and set aside.

2 Add the artichokes, garlic and shallots, and cook, stirring frequently, until the artichokes and garlic begin to brown slightly.

3 Season with salt and black pepper to taste and stir in the water. Cover and cook for another 8–10 minutes, shaking the pan occasionally.

4 Uncover the pan, increase the heat and cook for 5–6 minutes, until all the moisture has evaporated and the artichokes are tender.

5 In another frying pan, melt the remaining butter in the olive oil. Add the white breadcrumbs and fry over medium heat, stirring frequently, until crisp and golden. Stir in the chopped parsley and the reserved cooked bacon or pancetta.

6 Combine the artichokes with the breadcrumb mixture, mixing well. Adjust the seasoning if necessary, then turn into a warmed serving dish. Serve immediately.

COOK'S TIP Do not peel the artichokes too much in advance, as they discolour quickly on exposure to air. If necessary, drop them into a bowl of acidulated water. Alternatively, scrub them well and use with the skins still on.

There is nothing quite like the fragrance and flavour of rare Italian white truffles.

TAGLIARINI with WHITE TRUFFLE

INGREDIENTS
serves four

350g | 12oz fresh tagliarini

75g | 3oz | 6 tbsp butter, diced

60ml | 4 tbsp freshly grated Parmesan cheese

freshly grated nutmeg

1 small white truffle, about 25–40g | 1–1¹/₂oz

salt and ground black pepper

1 Bring a large pan of slightly salted water to the boil and cook the pasta until it is al dente. Immediately, drain it well and tip it into a large, warmed bowl.

2 Add the diced butter, grated Parmesan and a little freshly grated nutmeg. Season with salt and pepper to taste. Toss well until all the strands are coated in melted butter.

3 Divide the pasta equally among four warmed, individual bowls and shave paper-thin slivers of the white truffle on top. Serve immediately.

COOK'S TIP It is worth tracking down fresh black or white truffles. Store fresh truffles at room temperature – keeping them with your eggs is a good way of sharing their musty aroma. Truffle shavings or truffle oil should only be added towards the end of cooking to preserve their full flavour.

VARIATION Since no one has managed to cultivate truffles, they remain rare and expensive. If you can't find the real thing try canned or bottled truffles. Preserved truffles are less flavoured and benefit from a drop or two of truffle oil. Never be tempted to add more than a few drops – if too much of this precious oil is used, it will impart a bitter taste.

This is a richly satisfying dish, combining sweet Spanish onions, pine nuts and Parmesan.

PASTA with SLOWLY COOKED ONIONS

1 Heat the butter and olive oil together in a large pan. Stir in the onions, cover and cook very gently, stirring occasionally, for about 20 minutes, until very soft.

2 Uncover and continue to cook gently until the onions have turned golden yellow. Add the balsamic vinegar and season well, then cook for another 1–2 minutes. Set aside.

3 Blanch the cavolo nero, spring greens, kale or Brussels sprout tops in boiling, lightly salted water for about 3 minutes. Drain well and add to the onions, then cook over low heat for 3–4 minutes.

4 Cook the pasta in boiling, lightly salted water for 8–12 minutes according to the package instructions, until just tender. Drain, then add to the pan of onions and greens and toss thoroughly to mix.

5 Season well with salt and pepper and stir in half the Parmesan. Transfer the pasta to warmed plates. Sprinkle the pine nuts and more Parmesan on top and serve immediately, offering more olive oil for drizzling on to taste.

VARIATION To make a delicious pilaf, cook 250g | 9oz | 1¹/₄ cups brown basmati rice and use instead of the pasta.

INGREDIENTS
serves four

30ml | 2 tbsp butter

15ml1 tbsp extra virgin olive oil, plus more for drizzling (optional)

500g | 1¹/₄lb Spanish (Bermuda) onions, halved and thinly sliced

5–10ml1–2 tsp balsamic vinegar

400–500g | 14oz–1¹/₄lb cavolo nero, spring greens, kale or Brussels sprout tops, shredded

400–500g | 14oz–1¹/₄lb dried pasta (such as penne or fusilli)

75gl | 13oz | 1 cup freshly grated Parmesan cheese

120ml | 4fl oz | ¹/₂ cup pine nuts, toasted

salt and ground black pepper

hot and tasty

The onset of colder weather sharpens appetites for satisfying main courses. Try the ultimate fish pie, with a golden potato crust and chunks of cod and haddock, or mark the end of the barbecue season with fabulous hickory-smoked whole chicken with butternut pesto. Hearty stews are filling and delicious, and roasted meats and seasonal game birds make the perfect Sunday lunch.

The ultimate fish pie. Breaking through the golden potato crust reveals perfectly cooked chunks of cod swathed in a creamy parsley sauce. Cook in a big dish and bring triumphantly to the table.

FABULOUS FISH PIE with SAFFRON MASH

INGREDIENTS
serves six

750ml | 1¼ pints | 3 cups milk

1 onion, chopped

1 bay leaf

2–3 peppercorns

450g | 1lb each of fresh cod fillet and smoked haddock fillet, skin on

350g | 12oz cooked tiger prawns (shrimp), shelled, with tails left on

75g | 3oz | 6 tbsp butter

75g | 3oz | ⅔ cups plain (all-purpose) flour

60ml | 4 tbsp chopped fresh parsley

salt and ground black pepper

for the saffron mash

1.3kg | 3lb floury potatoes, peeled

large pinch saffron threads, soaked in 45ml | 3 tbsp hot water

75g | 3oz | 6 tbsp butter

250ml | 8fl oz | 1 cup milk

45ml | 3 tbsp chopped fresh dill plus extra dill sprigs to garnish

1 Put the milk, onion, bay leaf and peppercorns into a large pan. Bring to the boil, then simmer for about 10 minutes. Set aside.

2 Lay the cod and haddock fillets, skin-side up, in a roasting pan. Strain over the milk and simmer for 5–7 minutes on the hob (stovetop) until just opaque. Lift the fish out of the milk and transfer to a plate. Reserve the milk.

3 When the fish is cool enough to handle, pull off the skin and flake the flesh into large pieces, removing any bones. Transfer to a large bowl and add the shelled prawns.

4 Melt the butter in a small pan. Stir in the flour and cook for a minute or so, then gradually stir in the flavoured milk from the roasting pan until you achieve a smooth consistency. Whisk well and simmer gently for 15 minutes until thick and a little reduced, then taste and season with salt and pepper. Stir in the parsley.

5 Pour the sauce over the fish. Carefully mix together, transfer the mixture to a pie dish and leave to cool.

6 Preheat the oven to 180°C | 350°F | Gas 4. To make the saffron mash, boil the potatoes in salted water until tender, drain well and mash. Lump-free mashed potatoes are essential here; press them through a sieve to make sure they are really smooth. Using an electric whisk beat in the saffron and its soaking water, then the butter, milk and dill to make mashed potato that is light and fluffy. When the fish mixture has set, spoon over the golden mash, piling it on top. Bake for 30–40 minutes, or until the potato is golden brown and crisp. Serve immediately garnished with dill.

Everything is cooked in one pot – the chunks of fresh, flaky cod, made yellow with saffron, are added at the last minute, and their flavour is offset by the smoked paprika-spiced beans. Serve with a big pile of crusty bread.

COD and **BEAN STEW** with **PAPRIKA**

1 Preheat the grill (broiler) and line the pan with foil. Halve the red pepper and scoop out the seeds. Place, cut side down, in the grill pan and grill (broil) under a high heat for about 10–15 minutes, until the skin is charred.

2 Put the pepper into a plastic bag, seal and leave for 10 minutes to steam. Remove from the bag, peel off the skin and discard. Chop the pepper into large pieces.

3 Roughly chop the bacon. Heat the olive oil in a pan, then add the bacon and garlic. Fry for 2 minutes, then add the sliced onion. Cover the pan and cook for about 5 minutes until the onion is soft. Stir in the paprika and pimentón, the saffron and its soaking water, and salt and pepper.

4 Stir the beans into the pan and add just enough stock to cover. Bring to the boil and simmer, uncovered, for about 15 minutes, stirring occasionally to prevent sticking. Stir in the chopped pepper and tomato quarters. Drop in the cubes of cod and bury them in the sauce. Cover and simmer for 5–7 minutes, or until cooked. Stir in the chopped coriander. Serve the stew in warmed soup plates or bowls, garnished with the coriander sprigs. Eat with lots of crusty bread.

INGREDIENTS
serves six to eight

1 large red (bell) pepper

45ml | 3 tbsp olive oil

4 rashers (strips) streaky (fatty) bacon

4 garlic cloves, finely chopped

1 onion, sliced

10ml | 2 tsp paprika

5ml | 1 tsp hot pimentón (smoked Spanish paprika)

large pinch of saffron threads soaked in 45ml | 3 tbsp hot water

400g | 14oz jar Spanish butter (lima) beans (judias del barco or judias blancas guisadas) or canned haricot (navy) beans, drained and rinsed

about 600ml | 1 pint | 2 1/2 cups fish stock, or water and 60ml/4 tbsp Thai fish sauce

6 plum tomatoes, quartered

350g | 12oz fresh skinned cod fillet, cut into large chunks

salt and ground black pepper

45ml | 3 tbsp chopped fresh coriander (cilantro), plus a few sprigs to garnish

This traditional dish of fresh autumnal mussels cooked with shallots tastes as superb as it looks. Serve with crusty bread, or potatoes, to soak up the hot juices.

MUSSELS with SHALLOTS and SAFFRON

INGREDIENTS
serves six

2kg | 4¹/₂lb fresh mussels, scrubbed and beards removed

250g | 9oz shallots, finely chopped

300ml | ¹/₂ pint | 1¹/₄ cups medium white wine, such as Vouvray

generous pinch of saffron threads (about 12 threads)

90ml | 6 tbsp butter

2 celery sticks, finely chopped

5ml | 1 tsp fennel seeds, lightly crushed

2 large garlic cloves, finely chopped

250ml | 8fl oz | 1 cup fish or vegetable stock

1 bay leaf

pinch of cayenne pepper

2 large (US extra large) egg yolks

150ml | ¹/₄ pint | ²/₃ cup double (heavy) cream

juice of ¹/₂–1 lemon

30–45ml | 2–3 tbsp chopped fresh parsley

salt and ground black pepper

1 Discard any mussels that do not shut when tapped sharply.

2 Place 30ml | 2tbsp of the shallots with the wine in a wide pan and bring to the boil. Add half the mussels and cover, then boil rapidly for 1 minute, shaking the pan once. Remove all the mussels, discarding any that remain closed. Repeat with the remaining mussels. Remove the top half-shell from each mussel. Strain the cooking liquid through a fine sieve into a bowl and stir in the saffron, then set aside.

3 Melt 60ml | 4tbsp of the butter in a heavy pan. Add the remaining shallots and celery, and cook over a low heat, stirring occasionally, for 5–6 minutes, until softened but not browned. Add the fennel seeds and half of the garlic, then cook for another 2–3 minutes.

4 Pour in the reserved mussel liquid, bring to the boil and then simmer for 5 minutes before adding the stock, bay leaf and cayenne. Season with salt and pepper to taste, then simmer, uncovered, for 5–10 minutes.

5 Beat the egg yolks with the cream, then whisk in a ladleful of the hot liquid followed by the juice of ¹/₂ lemon. Whisk this mixture back into the sauce. Cook over a very low heat, without allowing it to boil, for 5–10 minutes, until slightly thickened. Taste for seasoning and add more lemon juice if necessary.

6 Stir the remaining garlic, butter and most of the parsley into the sauce with the mussels and reheat for 30–60 seconds. Distribute the mussels among six soup plates and ladle on the sauce. Sprinkle with the remaining parsley and serve.

Tart apples, plums and pears make a fabulous fruit stuffing that complements the rich gamey flavour of grouse perfectly. The rosy colour of the plums looks fantastic with the fresh green leaves of chard.

GROUSE with ORCHARD FRUITS

1 Sprinkle the lemon juice on the grouse and season it with salt and pepper. Melt half the butter in a flameproof casserole, add the grouse and cook for 10 minutes, until browned, turning occasionally. Use tongs to remove the grouse from the casserole and set aside.

2 Add the shallots to the fat remaining in the casserole and cook until softened but not coloured. Add the apple, pear, plums and allspice and cook for about 5 minutes, until the fruits are just beginning to soften. Remove the casserole from the heat and spoon the hot fruit mixture into the body cavities of the birds.

3 Truss the birds neatly with string. Smear the remaining butter on the birds and wrap them in the chard leaves, then replace them in the casserole.

4 Pour in the Marsala and heat until simmering. Cover tightly and simmer for 20 minutes, until the birds are tender, taking care not to overcook them. Let rest in a warm place for about 10 minutes before serving.

COOK'S TIP There isn't a lot of liquid in the casserole for cooking the birds – they are steamed rather than boiled – so it is very important that the casserole is heavy with a tight-fitting lid, otherwise the liquid may evaporate and the chard burn on the bottom of the pan.

INGREDIENTS
serves two

juice of 1/2 lemon

2 young grouse

50ml | 2fl oz | 1/4 cup butter

4 Swiss chard leaves

50ml | 2fl oz | 1/4 cup Marsala

salt and ground black pepper

for the stuffing

2 shallots, finely chopped

1 apple, peeled, cored and chopped

1 pear, peeled, cored and chopped

2 plums, halved, stoned (pitted) and chopped

large pinch of allspice

Whole chicken smoked over hickory wood chips acquires a perfectly tanned skin and succulent pinkish flesh. The butternut squash roasts alongside it wrapped in foil, and is later transformed into a delicious pesto. The chicken also tastes great cold so, if your barbecue is large enough, try smoking two at once, for a delicious meal the next day.

SMOKED CHICKEN with BUTTERNUT PESTO

INGREDIENTS
serves four to six

1.3kg | 3lb roasting chicken

1 lemon, quartered

8–10 fresh bay leaves

3 branches fresh rosemary

15ml | 1 tbsp olive oil

salt and ground black pepper

kitchen string (twine)

4 handfuls hickory wood chips soaked in cold water for at least 30 minutes

for the pesto

1 butternut squash, about 675g | 1¹/₂lb, halved and seeded

2 garlic cloves, sliced

2 fresh thyme sprigs

45ml | 3 tbsp olive oil

25g | 1oz | ¹/₃ cup freshly grated Parmesan cheese

1 Prepare the barbecue. Season the inside of the chicken and stuff with lemon quarters, bay leaves and sprigs from one rosemary branch. Tie the legs together with kitchen string (twine) and rub the bird all over with the oil. Season the skin lightly.

2 To prepare the butternut squash for the pesto cut it into eight pieces and lay them on a piece of double foil. Season well and sprinkle with the garlic and thyme leaves. Drizzle over 15ml/1 tbsp of the olive oil and a sprinkling of water. Bring the sides of the foil up to completely enclose the squash and secure the parcel.

3 Once the flames have died down, rake the hot coals to one side and insert a drip tray filled with water beside them. Position an oiled grill rack over the coals to heat. When the coals are hot, or covered with a light coating of ash, place the chicken on the grill rack above the drip tray, with the squash next to it, over the coals. Cover the barbeque with a lid or tented heavy-duty foil. Cook the squash for 35 minutes, or until tender.

4 Drain the hickory chips, carefully add a handful to the coals and replace the lid. Cook the chicken for 1–1¹/₄ hours more, adding a handful of hickory chips every 15 minutes. Add the remaining rosemary to the coals with the last batch of hickory chips. When the chicken is done, transfer it to a plate, cover with tented foil and leave to stand for 10 minutes.

5 Unwrap the butternut squash. Leaving the thyme stalk behind, scoop the flesh and the garlic into a food processor. Pulse until the mixture forms a thick purée. Add the Parmesan, and then the remaining oil, pulsing to ensure it is well combined. Spoon into a bowl and serve with the hot chicken.

Earthy and substantial, this is the ideal dish for chilly autumn evenings. The beans acquire layers of taste when slow-cooked in the rich sauce provided by the meat.

LAMB SHANKS with CANNELLINI BEANS

INGREDIENTS
serves four

4 lamb shanks

45ml | 3 tbsp plain (all-purpose) flour

45ml | 3 tbsp extra virgin olive oil

1 large onion, chopped

2 garlic cloves, sliced

1 celery stick, sliced

1 carrot, sliced

leaves from 2 fresh rosemary sprigs

2 bay leaves

175ml | 6fl oz | 3/4 cup white wine

30ml | 2 tbsp tomato purée (paste)

225g | 8oz | 1 cup dried cannellini beans, soaked overnight in water to cover

150ml | 1/4 pint | 2/3 cups hot water

salt and ground black pepper

1 Preheat the oven to 160°C | 325°F | Gas 3. Season the lamb shanks and coat them lightly in flour. Heat the oil in a large flameproof casserole over a high heat and brown the pieces of meat on all sides. Lift them out and set them aside.

2 Add the onion to the oil remaining in the casserole and sauté gently. As soon as it is light golden, stir in the garlic, celery, carrot, rosemary and bay leaves.

3 Put the meat back in the pan and pour the wine slowly over it. Let it bubble and reduce, then stir in the tomato purée diluted in about 450ml | 3/4 pint | scant 2 cups of hot water. Drain the soaked beans and add them to the pan with black pepper to taste. Mix well. Cover the casserole, transfer it to the oven and bake for 1 hour. Stir in salt to taste and add the hot water. Cover and cook for 1 hour more, or until tender.

Roasts make great Sunday lunches because they require minimum attention once they are in the oven, so the cook can relax with the family or friends.

STUFFED LOIN of PORK with APPLE SAUCE

1 Preheat oven to 220°C | 425°F | Gas 7. Heat the oil in a large pan and cook the leeks until softened. Stir in the apricots, dates, breadcrumbs, eggs and thyme, and season with salt and pepper.

2 Lay the pork skin-side up and use a sharp knife to score the rind crossways. Turn the meat over and cut down the centre of the joint to within 1cm | ¹/₂in of the rind and fat, then work from the middle outwards towards one side, cutting most of the meat off the rind, keeping a 1cm | ¹/₂in layer of meat on top of the rind. Cut to within 2.5cm | 1in of the side of the joint. Repeat on the other side of the joint.

3 Spoon half the stuffing over the joint, then fold the meat over it. Tie the joint back into its original shape, then place in a roasting tin and rub the skin liberally with salt. Roast for 40 minutes, then reduce the oven temperature to 190°C | 375C°F | Gas 5 and cook for a further 1¹/₂ hours, or until the meat is tender and cooked through. When cooked, cover the meat closely with foil and leave to stand in a warm place for 10 minutes before carving.

4 Meanwhile, shape the remaining stuffing into walnut-sized balls. Arrange on a tray, cover with clear film and chill until 20 minutes before the pork is cooked. Then add the stuffing balls to the roasting tin and baste them with the cooking juices from the meat.

5 To make the apple sauce, peel, core and chop the apples, then place them in a small pan with the cider or water and cook for 5–10 minutes, stirring occasionally, or until very soft. Beat well or process in a blender to make smooth apple sauce. Beat in the butter and sugar, adding a little more sugar to taste, if required.

INGREDIENTS
serves six

15ml | 1 tbsp light olive oil

2 leeks, chopped

150g | 5oz | ²/₃ cup ready-to-eat dried apricots, chopped

150g | 5oz | 1 cup dried dates, stoned (pitted) and chopped

75g | 3oz | 1¹/₂ cups fresh white breadcrumbs

2 eggs, beaten

15ml | 1 tbsp fresh thyme leaves

1.5kg | 3¹/₃lb boned loin of pork

salt and ground black pepper

for the apple sauce

450g | 1lb cooking apples

30ml | 2 tbsp cider or water

25g | 1oz | 2 tbsp butter

about 25g | 1oz | 2 tbsp caster (superfine) sugar

This hearty stew is both tasty and colourful. The combination of the spicy meat and sweet peppers is sure to warm you as the autumn winds begin to blow outside. Serve with plenty of mashed potato.

SPICY SAUSAGE and PEPPER STEW

1 Halve and seed the peppers and cut them into quarters. Heat the olive oil in a large heavy pan, add the peppers and sauté them over a medium heat for 10–15 minutes until they start to brown.

2 Meanwhile, slice the sausages into bitesize chunks. Carefully tip the hot olive oil into a frying pan. Add the sausages and fry them briefly, turning them frequently, to get rid of the excess fat but not to cook them. As soon as they are brown, remove the sausages from the pan with a slotted spoon and drain them on a plate lined with kitchen paper.

3 Add the tomatoes, sausages and herbs to the peppers. Stir in the water and season with salt and pepper, then cover the pan and cook gently for about 30 minutes. Mix in the parsley and serve.

VARIATION If you prefer, you can stir in the parsley, spread the mixture in a medium baking dish and bake it in an oven preheated to 180°C|350°F|Gas 4. Cook for about 40 minutes, stirring occasionally and adding more hot water when needed.

COOK'S TIP The peppers used in this recipe are the elongated, sweet yellow and red ones. However, you can also use elongated green peppers or a mixture of the bell-shaped red, green and yellow peppers that are more commonly found.

INGREDIENTS
serves four

675g | 1½lb sweet peppers

75ml | 5 tbsp extra virgin olive oil

500g | 1¼lb spicy sausages (Italian garlic sausages, merguez or Toulouse)

400g | 14oz tomatoes, roughly sliced

5ml | 1 tsp dried oregano or 10ml/2 tsp chopped fresh thyme

150ml | ¼ pint | ⅔ cup hot water

45ml | 3 tbsp chopped flat leaf parsley

salt and ground black pepper

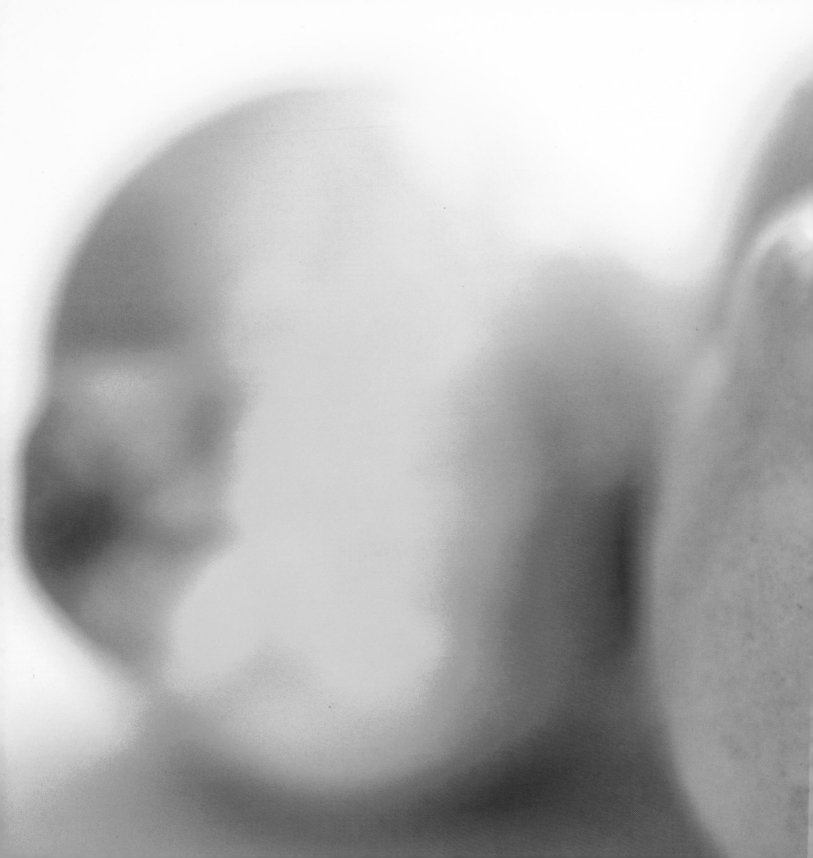

abundant and fruity

Autumn's generous harvest of fruit and nuts from the
woods and hedgerows provides the basis for jellies
and chutneys, as well as for intensely flavoured and
satisfying desserts. Enjoy the traditional combination
of blackberry and apple in a hot pudding, the crispness
of fresh hazelnuts in a mouthwatering tart, and mark a
special occasion with an indulgent dessert of pears
flavoured with cloves, coffee and maple syrup.

If you use eating apples bursting with flavour, loads of butter and sugar and make your own shortcrust pastry, then an apple pie can't go wrong. However, adding a buttery caramel to the apples takes it one step further and, coupled with the mixed spice, gives a rich flavour to the juices in the pie.

DEEP DISH APPLE PIE

INGREDIENTS
serves six

900g | 2lb eating apples

75g | 3oz | 6 tbsp unsalted (sweet) butter

45–60ml | 3–4 tbsp demerara (raw) sugar

3 cloves

2.5ml | 1/2 tsp mixed (apple pie) spice

for the pastry

250g | 9oz | 2 1/4 cups plain (all-purpose) flour

pinch of salt

50g | 2oz | 1/4 cup lard or white cooking fat, chilled and diced

75g | 3oz | 6 tbsp unsalted (sweet) butter, chilled and diced

30–45ml | 2–3 tbsp chilled water

a little milk, for brushing

caster (superfine) sugar, for dredging

clotted cream, ice cream or double (heavy) cream, to serve

1 Preheat the oven to 200°C | 400°F | Gas 6. Make the pastry first. Sift together the flour and salt into a bowl. Rub in the lard or fat and butter until the mixture resembles fine breadcrumbs. Stir in enough chilled water to bring the pastry together. Knead lightly, then wrap in clear film (plastic wrap) and chill for 30 minutes.

2 To make the filling, peel, core and thickly slice the apples. Melt the butter in a frying pan, add the sugar and cook for 3–4 minutes, allowing it to melt and caramelize. Add the apples and stir around to coat. Cook over a brisk heat until the apples take on a little colour, add the spices and tip out into a bowl to cool slightly.

3 Divide the pastry in two and, on a lightly floured surface, roll out into two rounds that will easily fit a deep 23cm | 9in pie plate. Line the plate with one round of pastry. Spoon in the cooled filling and mound up in the centre. Cover the apples with the remaining pastry, sealing and crimping the edges. Make a 5cm | 2in long slit through the top of the pastry to allow the steam to escape. Brush the pie with milk and dredge with caster sugar.

4 Place the pie on a baking sheet and bake in the oven for 25–35 minutes until golden and firm. Serve with clotted cream, ice cream or double cream.

This perennial favourite is a great way to take advantage of the season's apple harvest. There are any number of local apple varieties, so this cake will always be unique.

COUNTRY APPLE CAKE

INGREDIENTS
makes one 18cm/7in cake

115g | 4oz | 1/2 cup soft non-hydrogenated margarine

115g | 4oz | 1/2 cup unrefined soft light brown sugar or rapadura

2 eggs, beaten

115g | 4oz | 1 cup self-raising (self-rising) flour, sifted

50g | 2oz | 1/2 cup rice flour

5ml | 1 tsp baking powder

10ml | 2 tsp mixed (apple pie) spice

1 cooking apple, cored and chopped

115g | 4oz | scant 1 cup raisins

about 60ml | 4 tbsp milk or soya milk

15g | 2 tbsp flaked (sliced) almonds

1 Preheat the oven to 160°C | 325°F | Gas 3. Lightly grease and line a deep 18cm | 7in round, loose-bottomed cake tin (pan).

2 Cream the margarine and sugar in a mixing bowl. Gradually add the eggs, then fold in the flours, baking powder and spice.

3 Stir in the chopped apple, raisins and enough of the milk to make a soft, dropping consistency.

4 Turn the mixture into the prepared tin and level the surface. Sprinkle the flaked almonds over the top. Bake the cake for 1–1¹/₄ hours until risen, firm to the touch and golden brown.

5 Cool the apple cake in the tin for about 10 minutes, then turn out onto a wire rack to cool. Cut into slices when cold. Alternatively, serve the cake warm, in slices, with custard or ice cream. Store the cold cake in an airtight container or wrapped in foil.

VARIATIONS
• Use sultanas (golden raisins) or chopped dried apricots or pears instead of the raisins.
• A wide variety of organic ice creams is available from independent dairies and supermarkets – vanilla goes particularly well with this cake.

Pears are at their best in autumn and, combined with other ingredients such as cloves, coffee and maple syrup, they form the basis of this indulgent dessert.

STICKY PEAR PUDDING with ORANGE CREAM

1 Preheat the oven to 180°C|350°F|Gas 4. Lightly grease a 20cm|8in loose-based sandwich tin (shallow cake pan). Put the ground coffee in a small bowl and pour 15ml | 1tbsp of boiling water over. Leave to infuse for 4 minutes, then strain through a fine sieve.

2 Peel, halve and core the pears. Thinly slice across the pear halves part of the way through. Brush the pears with orange juice. Grind the hazelnuts in a coffee grinder until fine. Beat the butter and the caster sugar together until very light and fluffy. Gradually beat in the eggs, then fold in the flour, ground cloves, hazelnuts and coffee. Spoon the mixture into the prepared sandwich tin and level the surface with a spatula.

3 Pat the pears dry on kitchen paper, then arrange them carefully in the sponge mixture, flat side down. Lightly press two whole cloves, if using, into each pear half. Brush the pears with 15ml/1 tbsp maple syrup. Sprinkle 15ml|1 tbsp caster sugar over the pears. Bake for 45–50 minutes, or until firm and well risen.

4 While the sponge is cooking, make the orange cream. Whip the cream, icing sugar and orange rind until soft peaks form. Spoon into a serving dish and chill until needed.

5 Allow the sponge to cool for about 10 minutes in the tin, then remove and place on a serving plate. Lightly brush with the remaining maple syrup before decorating with orange rind and serving warm with the orange cream.

COOK'S TIP
Buy slightly under-ripe fruit and leave them to ripen on a sunny windowsill for a few days – over-ripe pears go off quickly.

INGREDIENTS
serves six

30ml|2 tbsp ground coffee

4 ripe pears

juice of 1/2 orange

50g|2oz|1/2 cup toasted hazelnuts

115g|4oz|1/2 cup butter, softened

115g|4oz|generous 1/2 cup unrefined caster (superfine) sugar or rapadura, plus an extra 15ml|1 tbsp for baking

2 eggs, beaten

50g|2oz|1/2 cup self-raising (self-rising) flour, sifted

pinch of ground cloves

16 whole cloves (optional)

45ml/3 tbsp maple syrup

fine strips of orange rind, to decorate

for the orange cream

300ml|1/2 pint|1 1/4 cups whipping cream

15ml|1 tbsp unrefined icing (confectioner's) sugar, sifted

finely grated rind of 1/2 orange

The deliciously tart autumn flavours of blackberry and apple complement each other perfectly to make a light and mouthwatering hot pudding.

HOT BLACKBERRY and APPLE SOUFFLÉS

1 Preheat the oven to 200°C | 400°F | Gas 6. Generously grease six 150ml | 1/4 pint | 2/3 cup individual soufflé dishes with butter, and dust with caster sugar, shaking out the excess.

2 Put a baking sheet in the oven to heat. Cook the blackberries, diced apple and orange rind and juice in a pan for about 10 minutes or until the apple has pulped down well. Press through a sieve into a bowl. Stir in 50g | 2oz | 1/4 cup of the caster sugar. Set aside to cool.

3 Put a spoonful of the fruit purée into each prepared soufflé dish and spread evenly. Set the dishes aside.

4 Place the egg whites in a grease-free bowl and whisk until they form stiff peaks. Very gradually whisk in the remaining caster sugar to make a stiff, glossy meringue mixture.

5 Fold in the remaining fruit purée and spoon the flavoured meringue into the prepared dishes. Level the tops with a palette knife (metal spatula), and run a table knife around the inside edge of each dish.

6 Place the dishes on the hot baking sheet and bake for 10–15 minutes until the soufflés have risen well and are lightly browned. Dust the tops with icing sugar and serve immediately.

COOK'S TIP Running a table knife around the inside edge of the soufflé dishes before baking helps the soufflés to rise evenly without sticking to the rim of the dish.

INGREDIENTS
serves six

butter or non-hydrogenated margarine, for greasing

150g | 5oz | 3/4 cup unrefined caster (superfine) sugar or rapadura, plus extra for dusting

350g | 12oz | 3 cups blackberries

1 large cooking apple, peeled and finely diced

grated rind and juice of 1 orange

3 egg whites

unrefined icing (confectioner's) sugar, for dusting

The honey-soft texture and the sweetness of the walnuts makes this cake irresistible.

MOIST WALNUT CAKE with BRANDY

INGREDIENTS
serves ten to twelve

150g | 5oz | 2/3 cup unsalted (sweet) butter

115g | 4oz | generous 1/2 cup caster (superfine) sugar

4 eggs, separated

60ml | 4 tbsp brandy

2.5ml | 1/2 tsp ground cinnamon

300g | 11oz | 2 3/4 cups shelled walnuts

150g | 5oz | 1 1/4 cups self-raising flour (self-rising)

5ml | 1 tsp baking powder

salt

for the syrup

250g | 9oz | generous 1 cup caster (superfine) sugar

30ml | 2 tbsp brandy

2–3 strips of pared orange rind

2 cinnamon sticks

1 Preheat the oven to 190°C | 375°F | Gas 5. Grease a 35 x 23cm | 14 x 9in roasting pan or baking dish that is at least 5cm/2in deep. Cream the butter in a large mixing bowl until soft, then add the sugar and beat well until the mixture is light and fluffy. Add the egg yolks one by one, beating the mixture after each addition. Stir in the brandy and cinnamon. Coarsely chop the walnuts in a food processor, then stir them into the mixture using a wooden spoon. Do not use an electric mixer at this stage.

2 Sift the flour with the baking powder and set aside. Whisk the egg whites with a pinch of salt until they are stiff. Fold them into the creamed mixture, alternating with tablespoons of flour until the egg whites and the flour have all been incorporated.

3 Spread the mixture evenly in the prepared pan or dish. It should be about 4cm | 1 1/2in deep. Bake for about 40 minutes, until the top is golden and a skewer inserted in the cake comes out clean. Take the cake out of the oven and let it rest in the pan or dish while you make the syrup.

4 Mix the sugar and 300ml | 1/2 pint | 1 1/4 cups water in a small pan. Heat gently, stirring, until the sugar has dissolved. Bring to the boil, lower the heat and add the brandy, orange rind and cinnamon sticks. Simmer for 10 minutes. Slice the cake into 6cm | 2 1/2in diamond or square shapes while still hot and strain the syrup slowly over it. Let it stand for 10–20 minutes until it has absorbed the syrup and is thoroughly soaked.

COOK'S TIP The cake will stay moist for 2–3 days, and tastes even better the day after it has been made, provided it is covered with clear film (plastic wrap) and is not put into the refrigerator. Serve with with coffee or a glass of brandy.

Dark muscovado sugar gives this dessert its deliciously smooth butterscotch flavour.

BUTTERSCOTCH and HAZELNUT TART

1 Break up the biscuits slightly, put them in a strong plastic bag and crush them with a rolling pin. Tip them into a bowl and add the toasted nuts and the butter. Mix until evenly combined.

2 Press onto the bottom and slightly up the sides of a 24cm/9¹/₂in loose-based flan tin or freezer-proof pie dish that is about 4cm/1¹/₂in deep.

3 Whisk the evaporated milk and sugar in a large bowl until the mixture is pale and thick and leaves a thick trail when the whisk is lifted.

4 In a separate grease-free bowl, whisk the egg white until stiff. Whip the double cream separately until it forms soft peaks.

5 Using a large metal spoon, fold first the cream and then the egg white into the whisked evaporated milk and sugar. Pour the mixture into the biscuit case. Cover and freeze overnight.

6 To serve, sprinkle the tart with hazelnuts and demerara sugar and cut into wedges.

COOK'S TIPS
• Remember to chill the evaporated milk for a couple of hours before you are ready to make the filling. This will ensure that it whisks well.
• Ground and chopped pecans, walnuts and almonds can be used instead of the hazelnuts.

INGREDIENTS
serves eight

for the case

90g | 3¹/₂oz gingernut biscuits (gingersnaps)

75g | 3oz | ¹/₄ cup ground hazelnuts, toasted

50g | 2oz | ¹/₄ cup unsalted (sweet) butter, melted

for the filling

300ml | ¹/₂ pint | 1¹/₄ cups evaporated milk, chilled

150g | 5oz | ²/₃ cup dark muscovado sugar

1 egg white

150ml | ¹/₄ pint | ²/₃ cup double (heavy) cream

chopped toasted hazelnuts and demerara (raw) sugar, to decorate

These luscious pastries use the season's plum harvest to great effect. The minute they have cooled down, they are sure to be snapped up quickly.

PLUM and MARZIPAN PASTRIES

INGREDIENTS
serves six

375g | 13oz ready-rolled puff pastry

90ml | 6 tbsp plum jam

115g | 4oz | 1/2 cup white marzipan, coarsely grated

3 red plums

1 egg, beaten

50g | 2oz | 1/2 cup flaked (sliced) almonds

for the glaze

30ml | 2 tbsp plum jam

15ml | 1 tbsp water

1 Preheat the oven to 220°C | 425°F | Gas 7. Unroll the pastry, cut it into six equal squares and then place on one or two dampened baking sheets.

2 Halve and stone (pit) the red plums. Using a small spoon, place 15ml/1 tbsp plum jam into the centre of each puff pastry square, leaving a border all around. Divide the marzipan among them. Place half a plum, hollow-side down, on top of each marzipan mound.

3 Brush the edges of the pastry with a little beaten egg. Bring up the corners of the pastry and lightly press the edges together, then open out the corners at the top. Glaze the pastries with some more beaten egg, then press a sixth of the flaked almonds on each.

4 Bake the pastries for 20–25 minutes, or until lightly golden.

5 Meanwhile, to make the glaze, heat the jam and water in a pan, stirring until smooth. Press the mixture through a sieve into a bowl, then lightly brush it over the tops of the pastries while they are still warm. Leave the pastries to cool on a wire rack before serving at room temperature.

COOK'S TIP Ready-rolled puff pastry has been used here for speed and convenience. If you make your own, the squares should measure 15cm/6in.

This preserve is a great way to use up those small, hard fruits that grow in proliferation all over the countryside at this time of year, with the added fragrance of the last of the year's rosemary.

QUINCE and ROSEMARY JELLY

INGREDIENTS
makes about 900g | 2lb

900g | 2lb quinces

900ml | 1½ pints | 3¾ cups water

4 large sprigs of fresh rosemary

preserving or granulated sugar

1 Cut the quinces into small pieces, discarding any bruised parts. Put them in a large heavy pan with the water, using more or less water according to the ripeness of the fruit.

2 Reserve a few small sprigs of rosemary, then add the rest to the pan. Bring to the boil, then reduce the heat, cover and simmer gently until the fruit is very soft and pulpy.

3 Remove and discard the rosemary sprigs (it doesn't matter if the leaves have fallen off). Pour the fruit and juice into a sterilized jelly bag suspended over a large bowl. Leave for 3 hours, or until it stops dripping.

4 Measure the juice into the cleaned pan and add 450g | 1lb | 2¼ cups sugar for every 600ml | 1 pint | 2½ cups juice. Heat gently, stirring occasionally until the sugar has dissolved. Bring to the boil, then boil rapidly for about 10 minutes. When the jelly reaches setting point, remove the pan from the heat.

5 Skim the surface using a slotted spoon to remove any froth. Leave to cool for a few minutes until a thin skin forms on the surface. Place a sprig of fresh rosemary in each warmed sterilized jar, then pour in the jelly. Cover and seal immediately. Store the jelly in a cool, dark place and use within a year of making. Once opened, keep in the refrigerator and eat within 3 months.

COOK'S TIP The amount of water needed for this jelly varies according to the ripeness of the fruit. For a good set, hard, under-ripe quinces should be used; if the fruit is soft, you will need to add a little lemon juice and less water.

This is a classic chutney to make when the last tomatoes have refused to ripen. Preparing your own pickling spice makes it easy to add exactly the right amount of flavour.

GREEN TOMATO CHUTNEY

1 Place the tomatoes, apples, onions and garlic in a large pan. Add the salt. Tie the pickling spice in a piece of muslin (cheesecloth) and add to the pan.

2 Add half the vinegar to the pan and bring to the boil. Reduce the heat and simmer for 1 hour, or until the chutney is thick, stirring frequently.

3 Dissolve the sugar in the remaining vinegar and add to the chutney. Simmer for 1½ hours until the chutney is thick, stirring occasionally. Remove the muslin bag from the chutney. Spoon the hot chutney into warmed sterilized jars. Cover with airtight, vinegar-proof lids and store for at least one month before using. Wipe the jars and label them when cold.

COOK'S TIP Jars and packets of mixed pickling spices can easily be bought; the contents of these varies considerably, so it's worth searching for a blend you like. If you already have a large range of spices, it is better to mix your own blend to match the preserve you're making. Typical spices and herbs used include: allspice, pieces of bay leaf, cardamom pods, coriander and mustard seeds, pieces of cassia or cinnamon, dried chillies, whole cloves, dried root ginger and peppercorns. Tie the spices in a piece of muslin (cheesecloth) and add them to the preserve while cooking.

INGREDIENTS
makes about 2.5kg | 5½lb

1.75kg | 3 ¾lb green tomatoes, roughly chopped

450g | 1lb cooking apples, peeled, cored and chopped

450g | 1lb onions, chopped

2 large garlic cloves, crushed

15ml | 1 tbsp salt

45ml | 3 tbsp pickling spice

600ml | 1 pint | 2½ cups cider (apple cider) vinegar

450g | 1lb | 2 cups granulated sugar

INDEX